First published in Britain in 1988 by
Young Library Ltd
45 Norfolk Square, Brighton
East Sussex BN1 2PE

ISBN 0 946003 96 3

Printed in Hong Kong

There are two more Then and Now books

Anna Then and Anna Now

Seven-year-old Anna compares the farmhouse childhood of her great-grandmother with her own life in that house today.

Kathy Then and Kathy Now

Nine-year-old Kathy compares her seaside holiday with a similar holiday enjoyed by her own great-grandmother.

Josette Blanco and Claude d'Ham
Translated from the German by Andrea Dutton-Kölbl

STEPHEN and STEPHEN
THEN NOW

Twelve-year-old Stephen discovers an old photo album. It is full of photos of his great-grandfather's life in the city when he was a child many years ago. Full of curiosity, Stephen compares the pictures of days gone by with the life he knows today.

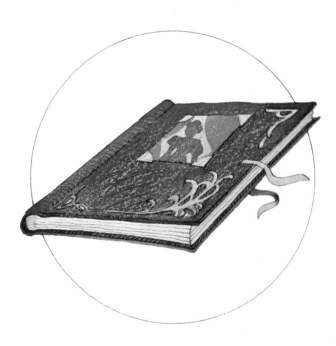

YOUNG LIBRARY

This is a picture of my great-grandpa when he was a child.
He was Dad's grandpa, and my grandpa's father.
His name was Stephen. He was twelve when this picture was taken.

Now this picture of Great-grandpa Stephen hangs in our living room.
My name is Stephen too, and I also am twelve years old.
My everyday life is a bit like his, but different too.

When he was a child Great-grandpa lived in a big city.
His family lived in a poor home that had no running water.
Great-grandpa's mother had to fetch water from a tap in the street.

Now I walk along the street where Great-grandpa used to live.
The trees and old houses disappeared a long time ago.
Instead of a tap there are parking meters and a telephone box.

In Great-grandpa's day an old tailor sat at his sewing machine,
and next door a cheerful barber shaved his customers.
Great-grandpa would look through the window and watch them at work.

Great-grandpa would peer through the window of this posh restaurant.
People would sit for hours over their lunches.
His parents were much too poor to eat here.

The tailor and barber have been replaced by a boutique
and a hairdresser. I can't see anything going on,
so the window displays are not very interesting.

They pulled the old restaurant down some years ago,
and replaced it with this self-service snack bar.
I come here with my friend to eat chicken and chips.

Years ago, horses were being replaced by motor vehicles.
Horse-drawn carriages, trams, cars, and men pulling handcarts,
all jostled for space in the cobbled streets.

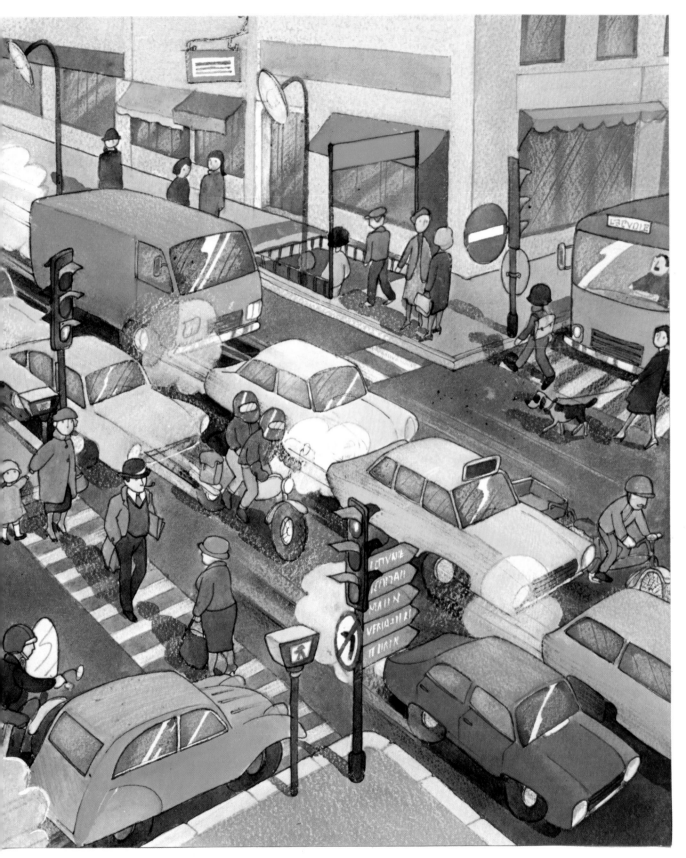

Today the streets are designed for busy traffic.
Traffic lights and one-way systems control the vehicles.
Pedestrian crossings and underpasses make streets safer for walkers.

Horses sometimes caused accidents.
This one is frightened by a dog,
and is kicking out.

The angry owner of a fruit stall
is showing a policeman how much
damage has been done.

Great-grandpa often saw mounted
policemen in the streets. Police
stations had their own stables.

We still have accidents today, of course, but usually because motorists are not careful enough.

This motorist is in trouble for parking on a double yellow line. He is showing his driving licence.

Horses are still used for ceremony and crowd control, but police now use cars and motorbikes.

Near to where Great-grandpa lived was a large laundry.
Washing and ironing was hard work for the women employed there.
Great-grandpa worked for the laundry as a delivery boy.

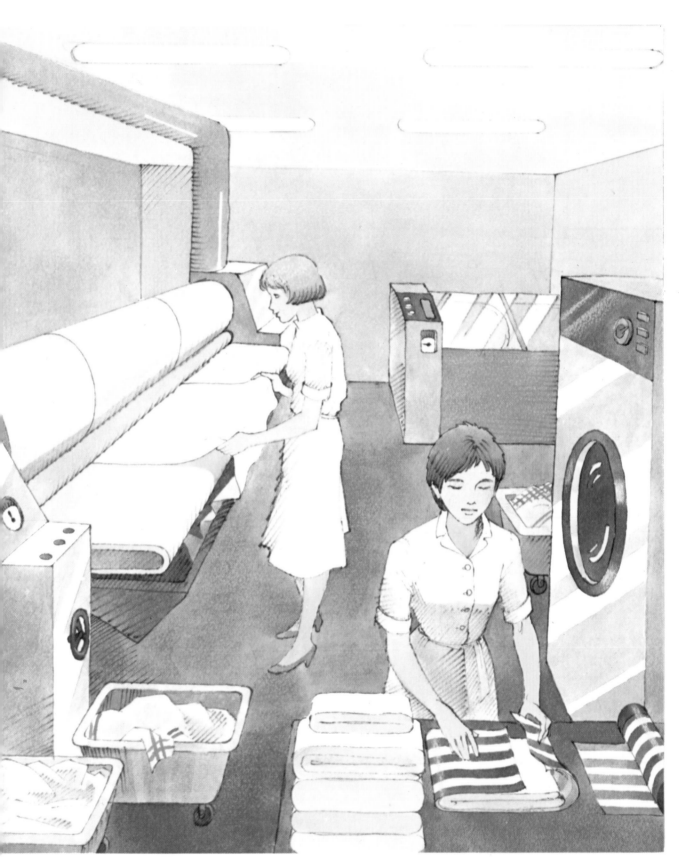

Today the laundry and dry cleaners employ only a few people.
Automatic machines do most of the work.
My mum does most of her washing in the washing machine at home.

In the olden days many children had to earn money for the family.
Great-grandpa delivered bread on Saturdays, and his friend
cleaned shoes every day after school.

Children could leave school at the age of thirteen in those days.
Most of Great-grandpa's friends had to start work
almost as soon as they reached their teens.

Like all my friends at school, I am given pocket money each week.
Some of my friends waste all their money on slot machines.
I prefer to go swimming, or watch the local football team.

The only work I do after school is homework.
But first I go swimming, or train with the school football team.
I have much more fun than poor old Great-grandpa.

Many of the streets were dirty in Great-grandpa's time.
On his delivery round, he sometimes met a poor man
searching through rubbish for something he could use or sell.

Today the rubbish is collected in automatic dustcarts.
Once a week I see a road-sweeper as it drives along,
brushing and suctioning up the litter with its noisy hum.

Great-grandpa would see pedlars and craftsmen walking the streets.
Bread, vegetables, meat, and groceries were delivered
to his door every day. The streets were always full of activity.

The haberdasher with his needles, pins, ribbons, and buttons,
went from house to house selling his wares.
The knifegrinder sharpened scissors and knives on his grinding wheel.

Housewives don't make their own clothes from animal skins any more.
Pots and pans are no longer repaired; they are simply thrown away.
The glazier only comes when he is called to replace a window pane.

I don't think my mum has ever bought anything at the door.
She likes going to the supermarket where she can pick and choose.
When her knives become blunt, she uses her own electric sharpener.

In those days people would dress up to go for a walk in the park.
Wealthy families employed nannies to look after their children.
A favourite toy was the hoop, which was kept moving with a stick.

It is still the same park but a lot of things have changed.
There is a playground for the little kids.
A track has just been provided for cycling and skateboarding.

My great-grandpa used to love going down to the river.
He would spend many quiet hours talking to the fishermen,
or watching the small boats bobbing past.

Further upstream, barges were towed by horses.
The horses walked along the bank, pulling on the tow-ropes.
When the current was strong the horses made only slow progress.

A new bridge, much wider than the old one, has been built
to carry the heavy flow of traffic. You don't see anglers any more,
because fish cannot survive in the polluted water.

There are still barges but now they are driven by powerful engines.
Great-grandpa used to wave to the bargees, but now
I wouldn't be able to see if anyone was waving back.

On Sundays Great-grandpa would go out for the day with his parents.
Once he had a terrific thrill — he saw
some daring men float up into the sky under a hot-air balloon.

My family also likes going out at weekends.
Last Sunday I got a very close look at a hang-glider pilot.
He took off from a nearby hill and flew right over our heads.

Great-grandpa Stephen enjoyed the music of the street musicians
The barrel organ played several new tunes each month.
People would come out of their houses to listen.

The organ-grinder also sold sheet music.
People played the music on the piano at home, and sang songs.
Often the fiddler would play, while his dog collected the money.

My friends and I like to hear music all the time.
We have cassette players with headphones so that we can listen
even when cycling in the street.

Our local record shop has thousands of records, cassettes, and
compact discs. I enjoy story tapes as well as pop.
At home the radio is on most of the time.

The merry-go-round at the fair was worked by steam, and so was
the barrel organ which provided the music.
Poor Great-grandpa couldn't afford the fair, but he liked to watch.

Last summer I took my little cousin to the fair.
All the rides and coloured lights are worked by electricity.
The taped music is played through loudspeakers.

Great-grandpa couldn't resist the smell of roasted chestnuts. Luckily for him a bagful only cost a penny.

Each evening the lamplighter walked through the town.
He had to switch on every gas street lamp with his long pole.
When Great-grandpa did his homework after dark he used an oil lamp.

I have never tasted hot chestnuts, but whenever I have spare pocket money I make straight for the hot dog stand.

Today we have street lamps which switch themselves on at dusk. We also have thousands of neon signs and advertisements, and everything in our home works on electricity.

Great-grandpa Stephen used to go on holiday with relatives.
A horse and cart took his luggage to the station,
then he travelled into the country on a steam train.

Last year my sister and I stayed for a fortnight with our grandpa.
Mum and Dad took us to the station.
The diesel train only took an hour to travel ninety miles.

Index

References are to pictures as well as text

Just for fun, did you see . . . ?
an aeroplane
a photographer
a sandwich board
some flatirons
a maid in uniform
and a bird in a cage.